Gracie —
one of the sweetest,
smartest, kindest, prettiest,
most kick-ass-est women
I've ever had the pleasure
to know — Happy 20TH

RAM

THE
NEW RULES
— of —
COFFEE

A Modern
Guide for
Everyone

JORDAN MICHELMAN
& ZACHARY CARLSEN
FOUNDERS OF SPRUDGE

Illustrations by Kelsey Wroten

TEN SPEED PRESS
California | New York

CONTENTS

INTRODUCTION

Coffee, You've Come a Long Way, Baby!

Coffee is nothing new. Humans have been enjoying it
steadily since the sixteenth century, and its origin story
goes back millennia. Chances are you grew up drinking
it, and have memories of how everyone in your your
family liked to take theirs—cream or no cream, maybe
honey, as a breakfast table staple or weekend afternoon
snack with cookies. But in the last decade something
special has happened to this age-old beverage: a new
boom of quality and entrepreneurship (embodied by
pioneering coffee companies like Stumptown and Blue
Bottle) has been met by a great wave of public interest
and enthusiasm, leading to an unmistakable new golden
era for coffee lovers worldwide. Coffee tastes better and
means more than it ever has. There have never been
more ways to drink it and brew it, and coffee's place in
our society gets bigger every day.

Wherever you live on the planet, chances are there's a
new place serving coffee in your neighborhood. That's not
an accident—it's part of something much bigger.

Thus, *The New Rules of Coffee*. We hope this book can
serve as a helpful primer to the wonders of modern
coffee, while paying respects to the beverage's past and

looking ahead to the future. Whether you're enjoying a pumpkin spice latte or a delicate AeroPress of rare, exotic Wush Wush (that's a coffee cultivar), it has never been a better time to be a coffee drinker—and a coffee lover.

We've spent the last decade at Sprudge reporting on coffee every day through stories big and small, from our homes in Portland, Oregon, and from cafes, coffee farms, and coffee festivals around the world. We work with hundreds of journalists all across the planet, chasing coffee stories wherever we can find them, and over the years, we've learned a thing or two about coffee along the way. We're sharing everything with you in the pages that follow.

With these fifty-five rules, we're dishing it all to you: from advice and travel tips to background information on what coffee actually is and why it matters now more than ever. And while we're sure this book will be responsible for kicking off a new coffee obsession or two, we hope above all else that it brings you a little bit of satisfaction, a moment of enjoyment, a chance perhaps to laugh and wonder—not unlike a nice cup of coffee.

1

RULES FOR COFFEE AROUND THE WORLD

Coffee is a fruit.

RULE 1 The roasted coffee product we grind, brew, and consume begins life as the seed inside a piece of fruit. The genus of flowering plant *Coffea* produces sweet red fruit, commonly called coffee cherries. The seed of that fruit—the so-called bean, which grows in the middle of the pulpy cherry like a tiny cherry pit—is what we process, export across the planet, roast, brew, and serve as a delicious, stimulating beverage. Your favorite cup of coffee started life looking more like what you might bake in a pie than what you might brew in a cup.

Coffea is a member of the taxonomical family *Rubiaceae*, a family of small trees and flowering shrubs. There are several species of coffee, but for our purposes we'll outline the two that are most commonly grown for coffee drinking: *Coffea arabica* and *Coffea canephora*. Arabica is what high-end, flavor-focused coffee has been built around, and indeed, the tagline "100 percent arabica" is still used to denote quality (although at really good cafes, this is naturally assumed and doesn't need to be shouted out). Arabica is fussy, prone to disease, difficult to manage, dangerously overplanted as a monocrop—and capable of producing absolutely incredible cups of coffee.

> Your favorite cup of coffee started life looking more like what you might bake in a pie than what you might brew in a cup.

Canephora is better known as robusta, its taxonomic *nom de brew*. Robusta is hearty, fights off disease remarkably well, is comparatively easy to grow, has twice the caffeine of arabica, and is somewhat less delicious—it has traditionally evoked the flavor profile of burnt rubber. That dark, automotive turpentine note you get in traditional Italian espresso? That's robusta. But in the spirit of this book, we should note that there are some new rules for robusta being written right now, as coffee agronomists and experts push the boundaries for improving cup quality in robusta around the world. Right now arabica is the specialty industry standard for high-quality coffee, but in another ten years, who knows?

Just like wine grapes, arabica or robusta plants have their own typicity and genetic diversity. Arabica can self-pollinate, and is capable of genetic mutation; in high-end coffee, more and more attention is being paid to the characteristics of different varieties of arabica plants in particular. Some major varieties of arabica include Bourbon, Typica, Caturra, and Pacamara, but there are multitudes of cultivars. Chardonnay and Pinot Noir have different flavor profiles and grow better in different conditions, and of course have their fan clubs. So do coffee varieties, and coffee drinkers can now fall in love with Geisha, which tends to have notes of floral jasmine; Pache, a mutation of the Typica variety first discovered in Guatemala; and even Wush Wush, a rare coffee variety first discovered (or perhaps first cultivated?) in Ethiopia, but growing happily today in Colombia as well.

Regardless, you're talking about a piece of fruit with seeds inside.

Coffee-Growing Regions, Typical Processing Style, and Flavor Notes

Coffee is a hearty shrub that can survive in a variety of environments—and can make for a wonderful houseplant! But the finest coffees are cultivated in the Tropics, the areas that hug the equator between the Tropics of Capricorn and Cancer. Tropical climates and high elevations are perfect growing conditions for top-quality coffee. There are outliers and there are places where lower-grade coffees thrive, but the coffee grown in East Africa, the Americas, and the Asia-Pacific are where most of the top-scoring coffee is grown, and that's much of what you'll find at today's high-end cafes.

We used to think of coffee flavor characteristics as being inherently tied to the world map, a concept popularized by Starbucks with its Coffee Passport program in the 1990s. Today this notion is antiquated; while there are general flavor characteristics for coffees grown in Kenya and Brazil and everywhere else, modern coffee farms have access to an ever-growing amount of information on growing, processing, and drying styles, which affect flavor far more than any national border does. As exporting becomes more transparent and easier to trace, coffee flavor characteristics can now be seen as a matter of microclimates and farm-specific conditions and practices, and should not be generalized. No two Kenyan or Brazilian coffee artisans do their thing the same way.

SOME OF THE PLACES AROUND THE WORLD WHERE COFFEE GROWS

Bolivia	Burundi
Brazil	Costa Rica
Colombia	Ecuador
Democratic Republic of the Congo	Ethiopia
El Salvador	Haiti
Guatemala	Honduras
Hawaii	Indonesia
India	Kenya
Jamaica	Nicaragua
Mexico	Papua New Guinea
Panama	Rwanda
Peru	Thailand
Tanzania	Yemen

COFFEE-GROWING COUNTRIES AROUND THE WORLD

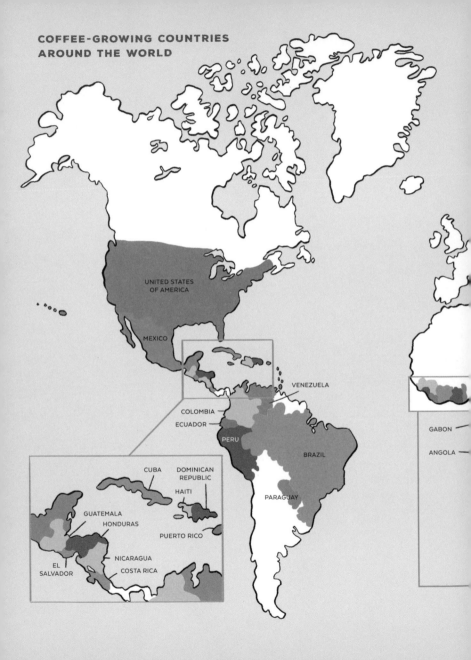

UNITED STATES
OF AMERICA

MEXICO

VENEZUELA

COLOMBIA
ECUADOR
PERU

BRAZIL

PARAGUAY

GABON

ANGOLA

CUBA   DOMINICAN
              REPUBLIC
              HAITI

GUATEMALA
HONDURAS
                          PUERTO RICO

EL
SALVADOR   NICARAGUA
                COSTA RICA

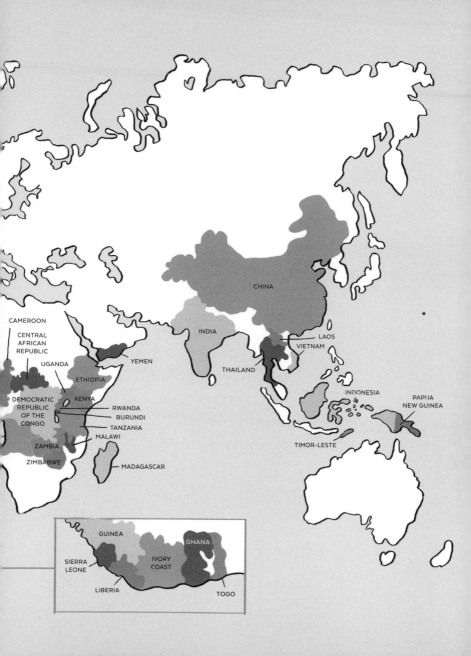

CAMEROON

CENTRAL
AFRICAN
REPUBLIC

UGANDA

ETHIOPIA

DEMOCRATIC
REPUBLIC
OF THE
CONGO

KENYA

RWANDA

BURUNDI

TANZANIA

MALAWI

ZAMBIA

ZIMBABWE

MADAGASCAR

YEMEN

CHINA

INDIA

LAOS

VIETNAM

THAILAND

INDONESIA

PAPUA
NEW GUINEA

TIMOR-LESTE

GUINEA

SIERRA
LEONE

LIBERIA

IVORY
COAST

GHANA

TOGO

Coffee is a global product.

Stop into your favorite local cafe and have a look around at the different coffees available. What do you notice? Ethiopia. Kenya. Colombia. Rwanda. In the cup it all looks like the same brown liquid. But we assure you, not all coffees are the same. Indeed, the network of agricultural commerce that makes coffee consumption possible in the twenty-first century is fascinating. If you live somewhere like New York City or Seattle there's nothing particularly locavore about drinking coffee—only the roasting happens locally. The rest of the process takes place on farms and estates thousands of miles away, where coffee is grown by farmers, carefully processed, purchased for export, and put aboard huge cargo ships. It is then delivered to the nearest major port before being sold as "green" (raw) coffee to your local roaster.

A thousand variables threaten the coffee's journey, and there are roughly one million things that can go wrong along the way, from infrastructure issues to shipping temperatures to a byzantine network of import tariffs. It's a miracle, really, that coffee makes it to our cups at all. Drinking coffee is one of the most global things you do each day.

Drinking coffee is one of the most global things you do each day.

Coffee's history is colonial.

RULE 3   Drinking coffee is also the most colonial thing you
do each day, short of putting gas in your car. Coffee
is a global product *because* of colonialism, and coffee's
history—its spread around the world, how it's cultivated, where it's planted—is intrinsically tied to some
dark periods in human history.

Starting in the sixteenth century, coffee went from
being a native plant of Ethiopia and Yemen, to being
a globally exported agricultural product tied to
notions of empire and a new elite culture of sociality.
The Dutch brought it from Ethiopia to their overseas
colonies in Indonesia; the French brought it from
islands off Madagascar to their colonies in the
Caribbean, including Haiti, where the coffee trade is
currently undergoing a resurgence; the Portuguese
brought coffee to Brazil, where its success helped
inspire large landowners to plant and cultivate the
crop across Latin America.

Coffee is a piece
of fruit that
grows far away
from its point of
consumption,
and many people
are involved along
its journey.

It's easy to think of this colonization of coffee as a sort of global game of crops, played out on some great Risk board of a world map. But what this ignores is the human element inherent in coffee production. Not only was the local agriculture of these colonies changed, but so were the lives of the people enlisted to produce these new crops. Coffee is a piece of fruit that grows far away from its point of consumption, and many people are involved along its journey.

For a deeper dive into this deeply challenging and troubling history, from dancing goats to thieving monks, we recommend Mark Pendergrast's book *Uncommon Grounds*.

All coffee is grown by a human.

We disconnect the human element from so much of what we consume—the food we eat, the clothes we wear, the books we read. This is what so much of today's modern culinary movements are rallying against, trying to reconnect us as eaters and drinkers to the people who source our food and wine, brew our beer, bake our bread. They're often people who live just down the street from us, or drive in from a nearby farm to set up shop at a farmers' market. The connection is palpable.

But coffee is often grown thousands of miles away from where it's consumed, disconnecting the coffee drinker from the coffee grower, and vice versa. Bridging this gap over the past twenty years is one of the central tenets—and we'd argue, greatest triumphs—of modern coffee. It's one of the big new rules we want to express with this book, except that it's not really a new rule at all. Coffee has *always* been grown by humans; it's just that now we're starting to treat coffee growers with the same esteem and respect we grant winemakers and chefs. It's a logical step to say, "If we care so much about how this tastes, then we should care about how it grows and who grows it too."

The connection
is palpable.

Coffee growers are artisans.

When we talk about crop variation, processing choices, harvest methods, and all the details that go into coffee production, it's important to remember that human beings in coffee-producing countries make these decisions. When a winemaker carefully grows, vinifies, and bottles an extraordinary wine, we call him or her an artisan. The same distinction should be made for coffee producers.

The distinction of recognizing these growers as artisans has never been more important. As coffee prices rise, and high-end coffee becomes more and more in demand, coffee's status among farming families and communities is starting to change too. What was once thought of as a crop of agricultural necessity among some of the world's poorest communities is now rightly seen as an artisan product capable of wondrous beauty and worthy of commanding a high price per cup.

When a winemaker carefully grows, vinifies, and bottles an extraordinary wine, we call him or her an artisan.

Whatever else you get from reading this book, we feel strongly that you should actively think and learn more about the people who grow your coffee. The same as any winemaker, farmers' market produce grower, or bread baker, these people are artisans, and their work brings our lives delicious joy.

The coolest cafes right now are in coffee-producing countries.

From Belo Horizonte to Nairobi, Panama City to Kigali, a new generation of coffee professionals are flipping the traditional script that says producing countries exist for resource extraction, and nothing more. There is now a brilliant crop of exciting new cafes popping up in countries known previously as places of coffee origin—and it's a trend that shows no sign of stopping.

Coffee has, for hundreds of years, been a product grown in point A, and then shipped to point B for consumption—a product inherently tied to colonialism. Unlike other consumables such as tea and wine, most of the best coffee grown is marked for export, and the coffee drunk by those who live near where it's grown is nowhere near as good as what gets shipped out. But this is starting to change fast, thanks to more access to resources, information, and a shift in coffee's cultural place in the societies where it is grown. There's no single factor causing it, but in our travels at origin, we've met young people who have learned so much about coffee via the Internet and through forging ongoing and meaningful relationships with the coffee importers and buyers investing in these communities.

RULE 6

> Unlike tea and wine, most of the best coffee grown is marked for export.

Every story is different, so here's just one: Our friend Gilbert Gatali, whose family fled the Rwandan genocide in the early 1990s, returned to Rwanda in the late 2000s to work on improving the quality of coffee exported from his homeland. Today Gilbert owns a successful coffee company in Kigali and is a fixture at international coffee events. His children will grow up in a Rwanda where coffee is not just grown to ship out; they'll be raised thinking of the coffee grown in their beautiful country as something valuable and respected.

All of this makes for better cafes and better coffee drinking in the countries heretofore only known for growing the stuff. Young people in countries like Colombia, Brazil, Kenya, Rwanda, and Indonesia are taking the beautiful coffees that grow near them and forging relationships with coffee farmers who give them unrivaled access to quality crops. Think of it as a kind of farm-to-table movement for coffee at origin—it's really exciting, and it means that soon you may need to visit a coffee-growing country in order to drink the world's best coffee, the same as you might visit Paris for wine or Taipei for tea.

No list on this topic could ever be complete, but we've featured dozens of cafes from producing countries in the last few years on Sprudge. Here are some of our favorites right now—all of which are spaces with modern design and high-quality service that offer a unique experience in coffee's backyard.

OUR FAVORITE CAFES IN COFFEE-PRODUCING COUNTRIES

PERGAMINO	Medellín, Colombia
OOP COFFEE	Belo Horizonte, Brazil
CAFE NEO	Kigali, Rwanda
VIVA ESPRESSO	San Salvador, El Salvador
CHIQUITITO CAFE	Mexico City, Mexico
MANGSI COFFEE	Denpasar, Indonesia
PETE'S CAFE	Nairobi, Kenya

Processing matters.

The bean we grind and drink is really the seed of the coffee cherry (see Rule 1). To get to that seed, coffee producers around the world use various tools and techniques to remove the fruit. Once the coffee cherry is ripe, the fruit is harvested—by hand in some places, by mechanical picker in others. Once a cherry is picked, its transition from fruit to exportable coffee product is a complex process. The way coffee is processed can dramatically affect its flavor. You might come across coffee in your favorite cafe or grocer that's labeled as washed or natural, and what that refers to is the processing.

There are two major styles of processing. Natural processing is the oldest way of processing coffee, and it's still practiced around the world, particularly in places where there are distinct dry seasons; Ethiopia in particular is known for natural-processed coffees. Natural coffee is processed by drying the fruit like a raisin, before it's hulled in a machine that uses gravity to separate the pulp from the seed. Natural processing relies on the right amount of sunlight and dry conditions, and when executed carefully, it yields a clean, complex cup. Natural processing needs far less water than its washed counterpart but needs significantly more patience and oversight to ensure quality.

Once a cherry is picked, its transition from fruit to exportable coffee product is a complex process.

The other major processing method is called washed. This is the dominant style of processing in modern specialty coffee. Styles of washed processing differ widely around the world, but all of them incorporate water in order to fully separate the flesh of the cherry from the seed before the seed is dried. Washed coffee uses machinery to depulp the cherry. A percentage of sweet, sticky mucilage is left intact and given time to ferment in water baths. The coffee is then dried and eventually the mucilage is hulled. This process requires equipment, access to water, and careful calibration and is thought to produce a more clean tasting coffee than the natural process. The end product of this process—the bean that will be exported and then roasted and brewed—is called green coffee.

There are several other methods around the world that incorporate some or part of the above processes, and many farms have begun experimental projects to test and pilot influence the tastiness of their crop. No matter the process, it's a critical component in how your cup of coffee will taste.

Washed coffee isn't clean.
Natural coffee isn't dirty.

Because natural-process coffees let the cherry and the seed sit in contact with each other for a long time, the flavors of the fruit do permeate the seed more than with washed coffees. Natural processing is deeply divisive among the upper echelons of coffee professionals, with some tasters disregarding the category entirely as flawed—if natural coffee isn't produced correctly, the fruit can rot rather than dry, and may leave undesirable flavors in the resulting coffee (we've tried cups with notes of rotten banana, and baby diaper).

Washed coffees immediately separate the cherry from the seed, eliminating the potential for this contamination. There's also something to be said for the obvious association between "washing" and cleanliness!

But if you like a little bit of funk, you might really like natural coffee, and natural process is enjoying a resurgence in recent years thanks to coffee buyers and roasters who champion this style for its low ecological impact and the expressive, delicious flavor it can yield in the cup.

RULE 8

If you like a little bit of funk, you might really like natural coffee.

Cascara

The coffee cherry isn't a very satisfying fruit on its own. You wouldn't want to sit down and eat a bag of coffee cherries on a hot day. Unlike a fleshy Rainier cherry, the coffee cherry is mostly skin and seeds, with a thin layer of sweet, tasty mucilage. In most parts of the world, the pulp is composted or thrown out. In places like Yemen and Ethiopia, however, the skin and husk of the fruit is dried and steeped with herbs and spices to make a unique, tealike drink. *Qesher* has been enjoyed by Yemenis for centuries.

Central American coffee producers like Aida Batlle of El Salvador experimented with this in the early 2000s and now sell dried coffee skin, or cascara, to importers. The dried fruit can be steeped like tea and has a distinct fruit-forward flavor. Depending on the quality of the coffee and the processing, it can take on notes of mandarin or jasmine, or hints of earth and tobacco.

Inventive chefs have started experimenting with cascara as a food product (look for cascara butter, cascara jam, and cascara flours in specialty shops), mixologists use cascara syrup for new-wave cocktails, and enterprising energy drink brands have expressed interest in it. Cascara is a trend on the rise.

JORDAN AND ZACHARY'S SUPER SPECIAL CASCARA TEA

— SERVES 2 ———————————————————

Little-known fact: When we launched Sprudge in 2009, we were hopped up not on coffee, but on cascara! Here's the recipe for the brew we drank that fateful day.

> 1¼ tablespoons / 20 g cascara (a generous scoop)
> 1½ cups / 350 g water, heated to 208°F
> Teaspoon wild honey

Combine cascara, water, and honey in a chemex or other heatproof glass container. Steep for 5 minutes, then strain. Serve hot, or cool to room temperature and serve over ice.

NOTE: Not to be confused with the herbal supplement cascara sagrada, cascara tea is sometimes sold as "brewable coffee fruit."

Darker is not stronger.

Blame marketing again, but that French roast coffee, long-roasted and dark, isn't stronger than coffee that has a lighter roast. It's not going to bench-press more than medium-roast coffee. This myth is particularly tricky, because no one seems to agree on how to define the "strength" of brewed coffee in the first place. Does strength indicate bitterness or strong flavor? Or does strength refer to complexity of taste? Is strength caffeine content? Or is it simply the ratio of coffee to water, dependent on the amount of coffee we put in the basket?

Are we talking about bitterness in the cup? If this is the case, dark roast will most certainly win. If it's bitterness you're after, the darker the roast the better. If it's strength of flavor complexity, we've got to award our friend the medium roast with the strongest brew award. Medium roast coffees will exhibit flavors found in the coffee itself (and not from the roasting drum). Medium roast coffee lifts up complex flavors. Darker roasts, on the other hand, will bring out bitterness.

No one seems to agree on how to define the strength of brewed coffee in the first place.

Caffeine content? That's going to be a mixed bag, as it will vary from cup to cup. Caffeine content depends more on the coffee itself and less on the roast. Recent research that indicates light-roast coffees contain

more caffeine than dark-roast coffees hasn't been fully vetted, and the truth is, the jury is still out on how much caffeine degrades during the roasting process.

Or is strength simply the concentration of the brew, determined by the amount of coffee you place in the basket? If that's the case, then it doesn't matter which roast you choose. A higher coffee-to-water ratio will be a more concentrated extraction (which also, regardless of how your beans were roasted, will result in a more caffeinated cup).

There may be times when one of these definitions matters more to you than the others. Have an early meeting? Maybe you want more caffeine. Or maybe you just like bitter-tasting coffee! But rather than getting caught up in debates about terminology, we think everyone should pay more attention to how the coffee tastes, and the story behind it. A little bit of brain over brawn might do this world good.

Acidity is a good thing.

Oh, acidity. So fraught, so misunderstood. Acidity is essential to the foods and drinks we all love. Have you ever bitten into a bland, mealy apple? It was probably lacking the malic acid necessary to give it that distinct apple flavor. Or maybe you've squeezed an old orange only to come up with a miserable, sickly sweet juice. The citric acid needed to give it zip was zapped. These acids and more are found in our friend coffee, too, and they're what make those wild flavor notes on the front of the coffee bean bag (blueberries, orange zest, SweeTarts, banana Runts, chocolate cream pie) possible.

People adore cold-brew coffee for its low-acid profile. In cold temperatures, the pleasant acids that lend unique flavors to coffee aren't as present or defined. While there are fans, many coffee pros turn up their noses on cold brew for just this reason. For many, acidity is what gives coffee life. Coffees that are under-developed and lightly roasted can be sour. Acidity without sweetness—think of sinking your teeth into a lemon—is horrific.

Acidity is essential to the foods and drinks we all love.

But when acidity is balanced with sweetness, it can be transcendent.

Why Roast?

The coffee beverage we all know and love comes from the roasted coffee bean. The unroasted bean is green, dense, hard, and unpleasant to drink. Roasting transforms coffee into a product that is easy to grind and delightful to drink—most of the time.

There are different styles of roasting and different roast levels. High-volume, commercial roasters can roast coffee in less than five minutes. Specialty roasters will take longer to roast coffee, taking care to monitor the heat and airflow to develop a coffee's intrinsic flavors.

Generally, coffee roast levels at the developed stage can be broken down into three categories: light roast, medium roast, and dark roast. Light-roast coffees tend to yield more acidity or sourness, and a thoughtfully developed light roast balances those flavors with a pleasant sweetness. Medium-roast coffees may have roast flavors with a little bitterness.

STAGES OF ROASTING

RAW COFFEE   YELLOWING

Dark-roast coffees will have almost exclusively generic flavors from the roasting process, with very little of the coffee's own flavor. Dark-roast coffees are great with cream and sugar.

In the United States, dark-roast coffee became a popular style thanks to the efforts in the 1960s of Dutch businessman Alfred Peet, and his students, who later founded Starbucks. Many of today's trendy shops (including Tim Wendelboe in Norway and Koppi in Sweden) have pushed toward lighter roasting practices, yielding coffees that some feel are more expressive of coffee's origin as a fruit. Many more work somewhere in the middle: not as dark as Starbucks, but not as light as what's popular in Scandinavia. Like all things with coffee, what you like best is really a matter of preference.

DEVELOPED

OVER-ROASTED

BURNT

2

RULES FOR
COFFEE
AT HOME

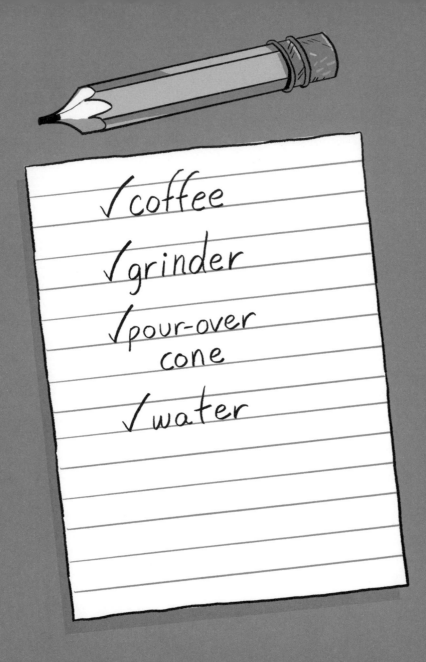

You don't need fancy gear to brew great coffee at home.

It's true, and hallelujah. To brew delicious coffee at home, you pretty much just need some version of the following four things.

RULE 11

GOOD, FRESH COFFEE. This part is totally up to your tastes—some people like dark-roasted, strong-tasting coffees, while others prefer coffees that highlight varietal and terroir characteristics, resulting in a lighter, sweeter cup. Make sure it's fresh (see Rule 17)! This is a huge part of making sure your brew tastes good. Decent, fresh coffee costs anywhere between $12 and $25 for a twelve ounce bag, which, considering it was grown by artisans on the other side of the planet, shipped by careful stewards across vast oceans, then roasted by another set of artisans wherever you might live, ought to seem like a steal.

A GRINDER. You'll need this because, yes, you'll be buying whole beans and grinding them yourself. This is key to making your coffee taste good, which is our goal, as opposed to buying preground coffee, which quickly goes stale and tastes bad. More spec-ifically, buy a grinder that uses burrs—two small pieces of abrasive metal, set at an adjustable distance, that crush the coffee beans as they pass between them—rather than one with blades that cut up the beans. Blade grinders look kind of like a

Good, fresh coffee costs anywhere between $12 and $25 a bag.

minuscule food processor—you may already be using one as a spice grinder. You can spend many hundreds of dollars on a nice electric burr grinder, or you can go with an entry-level option—the Baratza Encore retails for just above $100. If cost is an issue, you could opt to pick up a hand grinder like the Hario Mini Mill, which works just fine and costs around $30. (A nice bonus: hand grinders are small and portable and travel well on vacations, camping trips, or visits to Mom's house.)

A BREWING APPARATUS. This is pretty much about personal preference—we to love to batch-brew filter coffee (the electric coffee maker we all know and love) at home, because we're busy writing this book for you and don't want to individually brew each cup. Bonavita makes a totally fine 5-cup brewer for around $100—this brewer will evenly disperse temperature-stable water across your brew bed using a preset brewing time, and you can adjust your recipe by choosing how much water or coffee to add. Bonavita's home brewer is functional, but in our opinion, it's not especially beautiful. If aesthetics are important for your home kitchen gear, you might opt instead for a more attractive brewer from brands like Technivorm or Ratio. Both of these brands offer brewers that will evenly disperse temperature-stable water across your brew bed using a preset brewing time, just like the Bonavita—the major difference is that they'll look good doing it. Technivorm offers its Moccamaster home brewer in a rainbow of colors (one of this book's coauthors owns a Moccamaster in Millennial Pink). The Ratio offers a forest of different wood finishes, including exotic options like brazilwood. If you decide to go the hand-brewed route, basic brew cones from brands like Hario and Melitta start at around $10, while the AeroPress brew plunger is around $30.

A beautiful Chemex is more like $50 (it also doubles as a nice wine decanter and flower vase). We'll cover the pros and cons of automatic versus manual brewing later in the book, in Rules 23 and 24.

HOT WATER. Water science vis-à-vis coffee is a hot topic in the higher levels of coffee nerdery, but it stands to figure that, just as milk affects a mocha, the water you use to brew a cup of coffee will affect its flavor. Buying filtered water (or using a home filter such as Soma or Brita) is a fine place to start; if you want to go further, brands like Third Wave Water are developing capsules specifically designed for coffee brewing. You'll also need a way to heat up water. If you're using a home batch brewer, that step is covered by the wonders of automation. If you're hand brewing, of course the teakettle you already own and love is a fine place to start, but a specifically designed pouring kettle like those made by Hario, Takahiro, or Brewista reinforces good technique and hence, makes better coffee. These pouring kettles—called gooseneck kettles, after their distinctive spout shape—start at around $30. Worst-case scenario? You can always heat up water in the microwave, but you sacrifice a lot of control this way and can easily end up with water that's too hot or too cold.

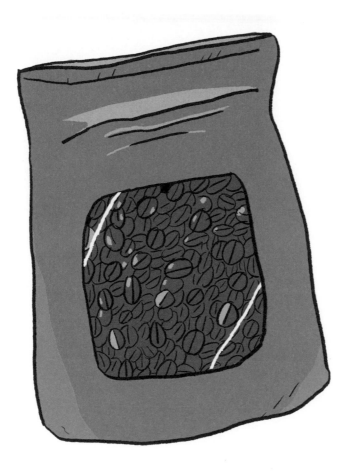

Coffee 201:
The Science of Brewing

You can pour moderately hot water over any ol' coffee grounds and call what comes out coffee. But we don't think you should. Making a great (or even a serviceable!) cup of coffee involves a lot of science, and the interaction between the coffee and the water can be affected by a lot of tiny variables.

Water temperature is important. Standard industry practice dictates that water temperature should fall between 195°F and 205°F. Water hotter than that can produce a bitter cup; cooler water can underextract the coffee. Avoid using water just off the boil (too hot!).

The quality of the water is just as important. You're looking for an acceptable range of calcium hardness, alkalinity, pH, sodium, and total dissolved solids. Some shops sell gallons of water with this ideal recipe. A company called Third Wave Water (see page 48) sells capsules that treat distilled water, creating what they claim is the perfect water for coffee brewing.

The chemical makeup of tap waters around the world vary widely—this is thought to be why bread tastes great in San Francisco, pizza is the best in New York City, and coffee brews so readily in Seattle. Coffee scientists have figured out a workaround by treating water using reverse osmosis and mineral additions, to create a molecular composition that plays best with the chemical compounds in coffee. But if you don't

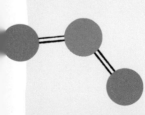

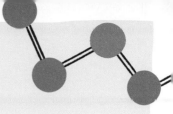

want to put on your pocket protector before your first cup of morning joe, just stick with filtered water and thank us later.

How you grind the coffee is a third factor. Burrs make for more evenly formed coffee particles, resulting in a more consistent extraction—if particle sizes aren't uniform, some will overextract while others will underextract. Overextraction leads to bitter coffee. Under-extraction leads to sour coffee. It's like putting different sizes of cookies in the oven: some might overcook, while others will undercook. An even approach is best.

Timing is everything. In pour-over methods, the contact time of water and coffee is controlled by gravity. If the coffee is too coarse, water will flow through it quickly, and the brew will be thin. If it's too fine, the water will be in contact with the coffee for too long, resulting in a bitter cup. There is no universally accepted grind size for home brewing—it's one of the most important variables in the whole process and can be frustrating. Trial and error is the only way to make sure you're doing it right, and small adjustments can make a big difference.

Good espresso at home ain't cheap.

RULE 12 The major exception to our previous rule—you don't need fancy gear to brew great coffee at home—is in the world of espresso. First, we can define espresso as a small, concentrated amount of coffee liquid, made using a specially built machine that quickly pushes hot water through ground coffee, resulting in a shot of espresso. It is *not* a different kind of coffee bean; it's a special way of brewing coffee. The entry-level cost for making quality espresso at home starts at several thousand dollars, and it's easy to go up from there. That's because the technology and degree of control that goes into high-end espresso machines is comparable to the kinds of tech you see in fighter planes and race cars; replicating this at home is not easy, nor cheap. Like audiophile stereo systems, wine cellars, and other such expensive rabbit holes, espresso is a hobby that becomes a lifestyle, and for some, an obsession that's never truly conquered.

Every part of the process costs money, and if replicating—or heck, bettering—the shot of espresso at your favorite cafe is the goal, you can't skimp on any

> Espresso is not a different kind of coffee bean; it's a special way of brewing coffee.

step. You need a real home espresso machine, first of all—quick-fix hand presses, gimmicky all-in-one brew contraptions, and pod machines don't cut it. We've done several comparative studies of home espresso machines over the years, and the cheapest we've featured falls at $975 for a serviceable model. You'll also need a proper grinder (see Rule 11)—a burr grinder with adjustable settings, preferably electric so you can quickly grind and brew multiple shots—and that's several hundred dollars more, and into the thousands if you go full nerd and opt for grinders with built-in scales, more exact grinding and dosing profiles, special stands for placing your espresso portafilter, and other assorted bells and whistles.

If you've got a $5,000 budget with room to expand and a lot of time to dial in the damn thing every day—tasting multiple shots, adjusting grind size, playing with other brew parameters—you stand a chance of making pretty good espresso at home. But it won't be easy, and it won't be cheap. For everyone else, well, we'll see you at the cafe.

You need to clean your coffee gear.

RULE 13

Everything that's good and true about our modern lives requires a cleanup now and then. Your car, your house, your clothes, your toddler—they all must be kept clean for maximum enjoyment. This is especially true with coffee equipment, and it's the thing home coffee lovers overlook the most. Clean equipment is part of why coffee at your favorite cafe tastes better than what you make at home—they clean their equipment at least once a day—and it's surprisingly easy to do.

Coffee is a molecularly complex substance (roasted coffee contains more than eight hundred volatile molecular species alone) and the process of grinding and combining it with hot water yields a plethora of sticky, staining residues along the way. Oils from the coffee itself cling to and gum up grinding gear (especially if you like dark roast), and scale dissolved calcium and magnesium salts from water—can form inside your brewing gear.

Roasted coffee contains more than eight hundred volatile molecular species alone.

Brands like Urnex and Cafetto sell cleaning products specially designed to combat coffee residue, and your local grocery store will typically stock these or comparable cleaning products along with filters and whole beans in the coffee aisle. Some cleaners involve grinding a special puck through your grinder,

to strip oils and restore functionality. Other styles of cleaner require a good, solid soak using formulations designed to break down scale and coffee residue. None of it is particularly expensive or difficult to manage.

It makes sense if you think about it: you clean your dishes and your glassware and your pots and pans, so of course you need to clean your coffee gear. Once every three to six months should work wonders. This is perhaps the simplest and most important rule we can offer to up your coffee game at home: you gotta keep it clean. Make cleaning a semi-regular part of your home coffee regimen.

Whole bean coffee is better.

Whenever possible, keep your coffee in whole bean form. Whole bean coffee keeps far longer than ground coffee ever could. Because whole bean coffee has less surface area than finely ground coffee, it holds in the vital aromatic compounds that give it life.

Oxygen and moisture are enemies to coffee's freshness, and ground coffee is fully exposed to these stale-inducing elements. Whereas good whole bean coffee will stay fresh and vibrant for nearly a month, preground coffee loses its luster in a matter of days.

We admit that buying preground coffee sure is easy and convenient, and even if the coffee doesn't taste good, you'll still get a caffeinated buzz. But keeping coffee beans whole and grinding on demand will enhance and lengthen the tastiness and your ultimate enjoyment.

RULE 14

Whole bean coffee will stay fresh and vibrant for nearly a month.

Pick a style of coffee you like.

RULE 15   Does it taste good? There you go, you've found your favorite coffee!

Honestly, it's as easy as that. Taste is the ultimate criterion, and taste differs wildly from person to person. We aren't here to tell you that some millennial with a man bun at the coolest cafe in your city actually makes the best coffee. If you want coffee to taste dark and strong, there are roasters that cater to that; if you're more open to lighter, weirder, tealike flavors that evoke flowers and ginger candy, a lot of today's trendy roasters are all about that. Most people are somewhere in the middle: they like a balanced, expressive cup that might taste good with pancakes and bacon.

Taste is the ultimate criterion, and taste differs wildly from person to person.

As you get more into coffee you'll learn, for example, that these everyday breakfast coffees tend to come from places like Latin America and South America. They tend to be washed (see Rule 7), they tend to be arabica varieties like Typica and Caturra (see Rule 1), and they typically score around an 84–86 on the 100-point cupping table: they're reasonably good quality, but not top drawer. Every quality-focused specialty coffee roaster worth their salt will offer a coffee in this style.

From there it's up to you: do you want coffees with big, freaky, electric flavors that kind of blow your mind? Check out Kenyan coffees or natural Ethiopian coffees. Are you more of a dark-roasted Italian-style espresso purist? There are brands in the United States that cater to that, although some people feel strongly that this is an experience that requires a flight to Milan. Prefer the darkest hell-bean known to man, capable of perking you up for days? You might be a robusta enthusiast. May God have mercy on your sleeping habits.

If you're totally lost, that's okay too: the best way out is to taste stuff. See if your local cafes offer public cupping hours—cupping is the coffee evaluation process the pros use, and experiencing it can help you learn more about the roasting and preparation process. You can Google brands that look intriguing to you and order some to try in your home. It's okay to be attracted by nice design—a lot of times that means the brand cares enough to work with a good designer, which can bode well for what's in the bag (see Rule 18).

There's no silver bullet and we aren't here to pass on our flavor preferences to you. It's amazing that coffee offers such a spectrum of flavors in this day and age. Diving in to find what you like is part of the fun.

Coffee Talk

Like any rarefied culinary culture, coffee has its own language. And while the flavors in coffee are fairly subjective, having some familiarity with the canonical list of flavors and words used to talk about coffee is a good way to start learning what you like and how to describe it to people. The Specialty Coffee Association has a coffee flavor wheel with close to one hundred flavor descriptors. Common flavors for high-end specialty coffee include: caramel, chocolate, peanut, stone fruit, blueberry, cherry, jasmine, and citrus. A lot of these flavors are the result of the variety or cultivation of the coffee, or the roast.

When you ask a barista to recommend a coffee you like, think about these dimensions of flavor:

ACIDITY. Some of the very same organic acids responsible for making your favorite fruits taste the way they do are present in coffee. Citric acid gives coffee that distinctive citrus flavor, and malic acid can yield apple and pear notes. A lot of naturally processed coffees have bright, juicy fruit acidity. Dark-roast coffees break down these acids and they're less expressive and muted.

BODY. The mouthfeel of coffee is important, and brewing plays a big part in the final outcome of a coffee's body. French presses can give coffee a chewy mouthfeel and filter drip coffee might have a lighter body, almost like tea.

SWEETNESS. During the roasting process, caramelization and the Maillard reaction, which gives browned food its characteristic flavor, both lend a hand in a coffee's sweetness. Overcaramelization leads to bitterness and less sweetness, which you'll find in dark-roast coffee (which is why we like putting sugar in it!).

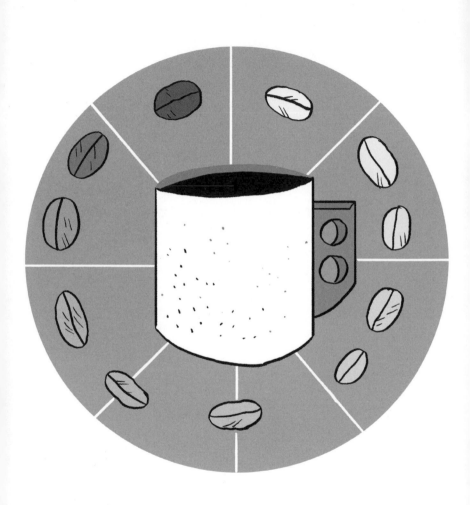

Roast profiles matter.

There's history and regionality in roast profiles. Alfred Peet made the West Coast of America fall in love with French roast coffee, and the founders of Starbucks took this method up to Seattle and beyond.

RULE 16

French roast is on the farthest side of the roast spectrum—it's taking coffee past the point of caramelization and carbonizing the coffee. You'll find flavors of unsweetened chocolate, burnt rubber, and spice. These flavors have little to do with the provenance of the coffee and more to do with the roasting process itself. French roast coffee doesn't have to be of high quality, and most of it isn't. French roast tastes really good with cream and sugar (and without them, we think it doesn't taste very good at all).

On the other side of the spectrum, you have light-roast coffee. At its most extreme, a developed light roast is tealike. Acidity is pronounced, and to many, the coffee is almost sour. You'll discover floral and fruit flavors in a light roast, and the characteristics of the coffee's variety, terroir, and process will be exposed.

In the middle, you'll find a happy balance with medium-roast coffees. Medium-roast coffees experience more caramelization than light-roast coffees and have a nice balance of sweetness, acidity, and some elements of roast flavors.

Some flavors have little to do with the provenance of the coffee and more to do with the roasting process itself.

You can't tell if coffee is fresh by looking at it.

RULE 17

Fresh coffee is a magical thing but its magic wears out rather quickly.

Ever find a bag of coffee hiding in the far reaches of your kitchen cabinet, not knowing how it got there or how long it's been there? Unless there's a date on the bag, it'll be difficult to gauge just how old that coffee truly is. The surface of whole bean coffee will not reveal its age. A freshly roasted coffee bean might have an oily sheen or a matte finish, just as an old bean might.

If you don't know when coffee was roasted, it's probably stale. Most coffees these days proudly display their roasted date (some even disclose when the coffee was harvested). It's rarely a good sign when the coffee bag has a best by date. Best by dates don't tell you when it was roasted—and many of these coffees say "best before" a year to two years from the date the coffee was packaged. That's a long time!

Stale coffee will generally be a shell of its former self—papery, thin, and deeply unsatisfying.

As with most rules, there is a tiny exception: some grocery stores require roasters to place a shelf life date on their bags. To make it extra confusing, and to meet this criteria, you might find two dates on a bag of coffee. Look for and rely on the "roasted on" date, and keep coffee about a month after it's roast, two months if you're desperate.

Without knowing the date the coffee was roasted, the only way to determine whether it's fresh is by grinding it, brewing it, and drinking it. When you grind the coffee, you'll notice right away if the coffee is stale. Fresh coffee is filled with volatile aromatics that escape into the air and fill your kitchen. Stale coffee does not do this.

Introducing water will also help determine the age: fresh coffee typically blooms—puffs up and bubbles—when you pour hot water over it, as carbon dioxide and other gases escape. Stale coffee has already released those gases, so nothing will happen.

The final method is drinking it. Stale coffee will generally be a shell of its former self—papery, thin, and deeply unsatisfying.

There are exceptions! We personally tasted a coffee that was six years off roast and kept in a dark, cool cabinet in an amber jar. The coffee was lifeless with no acidity but it was also incredibly, impossibly sweet. Would we recommend doing this? Absolutely not. But it's worth mentioning.

Fresh coffee lives in nice packaging.

RULE 18

If you come across a barrel of coffee with a scoop in it, steer clear! Those funky plastic bins in your grocer's bulk section? That's where potentially good coffee goes to die. Or at least get stale and bland. Freshly roasted coffee likes living in a cool, dark place. It doesn't like to be presented in a clear container, open to the light, repeatedly exposed to the air as patron after patron opens the bin, nor does it like rubbing up against a plastic bin coated in layers of oily residue from its previous residents. The best coffee is usually safely stored in tins or bags, portioned for use within a couple of weeks, and sealed from the air and light.

> Freshly roasted coffee likes living in a cool, dark place.

If you don't have the luxury of visiting your local roaster for a scoop of some freshly roasted stuff, stick to the prepackaged bags with a roast date in the grocery aisle.

Don't freeze coffee (but if you do, here's how to do it well).

RULE 19

Coffee is best stored in an airtight container in a cool, dry, dark place. This slows the inevitable staleness. It's not advised to keep your coffee in the refrigerator—neighboring foods and their aromatics will permeate the coffee—but on the rare occasion when you want to hold on to some roasted coffee, it is permissible to freeze it. Here's how.

Divide your whole bean coffee into portions and vacuum-seal them. That way, when you're pulling it out of the deep freeze, you're only doing it once. Allow the beans to reach room temperature before grinding. In smaller portions, the coffee should come up to room temperature rather quickly.

Neighboring foods and their aromatics will permeate coffee in the refrigerator.

Why preportion it? Every time you remove something from the freezer, condensation builds up as it begins to defrost. When you put a defrosted item back into the freezer, the condensation will refreeze, hastening dehydration and oxidation (freezer burn), which will negatively affect flavor.

Instant coffee is getting cool again.

Instant coffee, the late nineteenth-century foodstuff that's best reserved for consumption during wartime or in your post-apocalyptic bunker, is having a bit of a millennial comeback tech-disruption boom. This soluble coffee is basically brewed coffee that is dried and powdered—just add hot water and serve. For more than a hundred years, companies have been figuring out ways to maximize profits for instant coffee by using less raw material (coffee beans) in the base and more filler (like wheat, soybean, barley, and chaff, a by-product of coffee roasting).

Starbucks famously flooded the market a relatively a short time ago with its Via line of flavored and unflavored instant offerings. The general consensus is that instant coffee is bad. That is, until millennials figured out that you can actually make it taste good.

But how?

Just start with good coffee, brew it well, and carefully process it to produce instant coffee. It's not much more of a wild secret than that. Turns out, most of the commercially available instant coffee starts as low-quality coffee. By starting with a high-quality coffee,

RULE 20

Millennials figured out that you can actually make instant coffee taste good.

it's possible to make instant coffee that actually tastes good. We like Sudden Coffee, out of San Francisco, and Voilà from Oregon, but this is a product category that's changing fast, with new brands emerging all the time. Rest assured we'll be reporting on all of it in the pages of Sprudge—we see the emergence of delicious instant coffee as potentially being one of the next major coffee trends worldwide.

Iced coffee and cold brew are sisters, not twins.

We're temperature agnostic when it comes to coffee (except for extra-hot coffee, but we'll get to that later). Hot, cold, we like it all. What people can't seem to agree on is the right way to brew cold coffee.

RULE 21

The most common way to make cold coffee is by brewing a concentrate of hot coffee and then diluting it with ice. Iced coffee brewed in this fashion retains the crisp acidity and holds on to some of the fruit and floral components that come along for the ride.

In the last decade, cold-brew coffee has gained in popularity. This method uses cold water and coffee grounds. The two steep together for 16 to 48 hours. The slurry is filtered, and the cup yields a sweet, syrupy coffee with very little acidity.

Cold brew is having a moment. Investors see it as a new beverage category (much like energy drinks in the late '90s) and store shelves are stocked with bottles, cartons, and cans of the stuff. High-end bars are installing taps of nitro-infused cold brew that dramatically cascades into the cup, not unlike a Guinness.

Investors see cold brew as a new beverage category.

Connoisseurs call out cold brew for lacking unique characteristics, but they can't stop its momentum. Cold brew is here to stay.

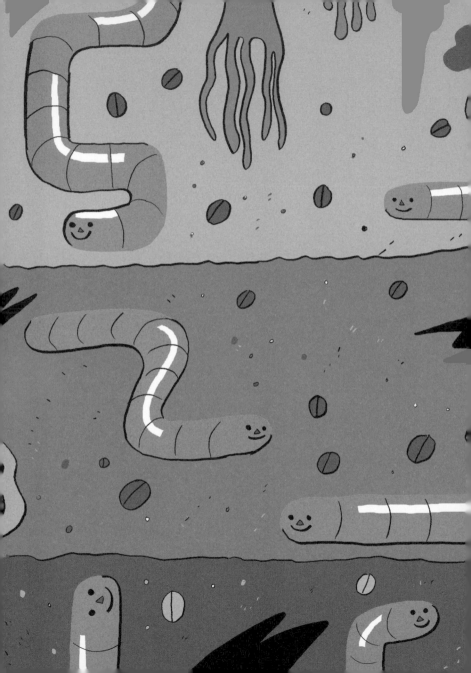

Coffee is a terrible thing to waste.

Don't throw the grounds out with the brew water. Your spent coffee grounds make a fabulous addition to your compost pile. That's because used coffee is pH neutral and rich in nitrogen. Worms love it—and your plants will too! If you have a large garden, many cafes offer their spent grounds to customers for free.

Composting coffee grounds for lush fertilizer isn't the only thing folks are doing with coffee waste. Companies are using coffee waste to develop textiles, inks, and paper products. Pioneering vermiculture (worm compost) work has been done using coffee waste by the American specialty coffee roasting company Counter Culture Coffee, based in Durham, North Carolina, which has living vermiculture labs in each of their dozen-plus regional training centers nationwide.

Used coffee is pH neutral and rich in nitrogen.

There's room for electric in home brewing.

RULE 23

As we outlined in Rule 11, brewing coffee at home doesn't have to cost a ton. And that's a good thing! But if making coffee at home that tastes good is the goal, there are many paths to get there. To start, let's talk about the first big choice you'll need to make: an automatic brewer versus a manual brewer.

Like most things in life, there are pros and cons to either choice, and what works best for you is ultimately a personal decision. A lot of people—your authors included—love the convenience and reliability of an automatic coffee brewer at home. These are sometimes called batch-brew machines in the coffee industry, because they do exactly that: brew up a multicup batch of coffee that's ready to drink in multiple servings. The exact volume brewed varies from machine to machine and is determined by how much ground coffee and water you put into the device before pressing the button.

> Automatic coffee brewers are sometimes called batch-brew machines in the coffee industry.

A range of quality home brewer options has risen up that focuses on consistency and temperature stability—the holy grail of coffee machines—and these two important variables can make them a preferable choice over the vagaries of hand brewing. Home brewers like those made by Bonavita and Technivorm range from $100 to $300, make consistently delicious coffee day in, day out, and look pretty cool on your countertop. There are even more high-end options emerging from brands like Ratio and Wilfa, which carry a higher price point.

There is something beautiful about having a well-made electric coffee brewer in your home, especially if you're the sort of person for whom the immediate delivery of caffeine is a prerequisite in the early morning hours. Home brewers remove many variables and unknowns from the brewing process, and allow you, in our opinion, to focus instead on how the coffee itself tastes. For what it's worth, we're squarely in the "batch-brew at home" camp here at Sprudge.

Manual Brewing Methods

If you decide to try manual brewing at home—and we think you should!—you'll need to find a method that fits your style. French press is popular for its relative convenience: you weigh and grind your coffee, put it in the press, pour hot water over it, wait, then press and pour. It's pretty hands-off. Other methods are much more involved, including individual cup drippers made by brands like Beehouse, Hario, and Kalita. In this method, a single cup's worth of coffee is weighed and ground, and then placed into a paper filter that rests inside a cradle (often cone-shaped, sometimes shaped like a trough, it depends on the device, and coffee nerds argue endlessly over the minutiae of this). From there you carefully pour water from a kettle—your tea kettle works fine, but if you want to get fancy this is the place to use that gooseneck kettle we talked about on page 48 from brands like Hario, Takahiro, and Brewista, adding more water as you go over the course of three to five minutes.

BEEHOUSE DRIPPER

KALITA WAVE

HARIO V60

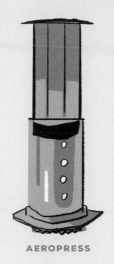

AEROPRESS

TODDY

FRENCH PRESS

VACUUM POT

CHEMEX

Manual brewing at home is a matter of devotion.

RULE 24

We just got done telling you that we love having an automatic brewer at home, but there are many pros to enjoying manually brewed coffee at home as well. This is how a lot of coffee professionals prefer to make coffee in their own homes, and we think it has something to offer everyone.

It feels as if we, as a society, have treated the coffee beverage as a helplessly, hopelessly quantified commodity. Coffee is literally traded on the stock market. The tendrils of its colonial narrative stretch deep, echoing some really shameful chapters in human history and calling us to account as consumers today. And so with that in mind, there is something delightfully and refreshingly analog about taking the time to intentionally, mindfully brew yourself a single cup of coffee at home. It's sort of like a big "F-you" to the $1 quick-cup culture all around us. (Not that there's anything wrong with the occasional $1 quick cup.)

> Manual brewing is sort of like a big "F-you" to the $1 quick-cup culture all around us.

Manual brewing requires a sort of focus and intentionality that sets it apart from other methods. It's just you and the coffee, with no outside force controlling the many variables that define the coffee brewing process. Did you pour too fast? Did you mess up your hand movements? Was the water too hot? Is the grind too coarse? It's like trimming a bonsai tree or raising a child: there are a thousand little things that can go wrong, and will, but when you get the process dialed in, the sense of accomplishment and pride is enormous.

Always consider the Chemex.

RULE 25   There's one home brewing method that we think
stands above all the others. Whether you're Team
Manual or Team Automatic, there is a place for the
Chemex coffee maker in your home.

The Chemex is a triumph of form and function. It is,
quite simply, one of coffee's most beautiful contribu-
tions to the wider world of functional interior design,
and it makes a tasty cup of coffee too. It was invented
in 1941 by German-born inventor Dr. Peter Schlumbohm, a true twentieth-century character and bon
vivant whose other, less popular inventions include a
portable Champagne cooling device and "unburnable
gasoline." His Chemex coffee maker was a hit almost
immediately, and went on to appear in James Bond
films, episodes of *The Mary Tyler Moore Show*, and
as gifts to U.S. presidents Harry Truman and Lyndon
B. Johnson. The Chemex is part of the permanent
collection at the Museum of Modern Art in New York
City, where it appears in a gallery installation alongside
other functional interior design pieces by the likes of
Charles Eames and Ludwig Mies van der Rohe.

Not bad for a coffee maker! Today the Chemex is
produced in western Massachusetts and can be
purchased new for around $50. We like hunting
for midcentury Chemex coffee makers at vintage

The Chemex
is part of the
permanent
collection at
the Museum of
Modern Art in
New York City.

interiors shops—you'll know them by the thickness of the glass. There's also, perhaps unsurprisingly, a wide range of knock-off Chemex-like makers out on the market, and sometimes in the very same vintage stores. The original is of a distinctly higher quality, so shop wisely and Google liberally.

The Chemex makes a tasty cup of coffee—you need to use the brand-specific bonded Chemex filters, which are designed for the unique size and shape of the cone and won't fall out during pouring—but if we're honest, that's not our favorite part. We love the Chemex for its endless versatility and have used our own personal stash of Chemexes as a wine decanter, flower vase, terrarium, fish tank, water pitcher, punch bowl, self-defense blunt object (long story), watering can, and when filled with dry ice and some glowing neon wristbands, as part of an elaborate Halloween decorative display. We think Dr. Schlumbohm, who affixed a series of gilded gold Chemexes to the side of his Coupe de Ville, would strongly approve.

Cute cups make coffee taste better

RULE 26

Have you ever wondered why a glass of wine tastes better in a fancy restaurant? Or why a cup of coffee tastes better poured into your favorite mug? The human brain is an amazing thing, and the way we encounter and process flavor is subject to the influence of a thousand variables. Writing in *Scientific American*, Yale School of Medicine neuroscientist Dana Small tells us that taste is "actually a fusion of a food's taste, smell, and touch into a single sensation." That means that no, you aren't crazy: today's pour-over really did taste so good in part due to what vessel you served it in.

Good cafes know this and strive to serve up their coffees in ceramics that are as lovely to hold as they are to drink from. Market Lane Coffee of Melbourne, Australia, has partnered with Roberta Gartland, a master ceramicist working in the medium of Tasmanian ice porcelain, which is soft to the touch and glazed a delicate blue green, to supply their cups. Patricia Coffee Brewers, also in Melbourne, works with ceramicist Malcolm Greenwood. The G&B Coffee/Go Get Em Tiger family of coffee brands in Los Angeles partnered with influential ceramicist Ben Medansky for their cups. Medansky is now one

> The way we encounter and process flavor is subject to the influence of a thousand variables.

NOBUHITO NISHIGAWARA

JORDAN'S FIGMENT MUG

BEN MENDANSKY

EDITH HEATH

MALCOLM GREENWOOD

of the city's most in-demand ceramicists, and his work has appeared in the Cooper Hewitt Smithsonian Design Museum and galleries around the world.

Nice cups are the secret weapon that help good cafes serve great coffee, and you can do the same neat trick for yourself at home. Like all art, your taste in ceramics will be subjective. Maybe you want to take home the same Gartland or Medansky cups found in these high-end cafes; maybe your taste is more toward streamlined midcentury mugs, like the iconic Edith Heath coffee mug design made by Heath Ceramics of California; maybe you're after that ineffable, hand-thrown, imperfect *wabi-sabi* effect found in the works of Japanese ceramicists like Masanobu Ando (Gifu Prefecture, Japan) or Nobuhito Nishigawara (Orange County, California).

Or maybe you're a little more simple. Jordan's favorite mug comes from the Figment ride at Walt Disney World, purchased in the gift shop at some point in the 1990s. Zachary's favorite mug comes from Ikea. You do you, just know that this stuff helps your coffee taste better, and think of it as part of what makes drinking coffee fun.

Coffee and food play well together.

Before, during, or after meals, coffee gets along wonderfully with food. We've been privy to some pretty avant-garde coffee and food pairings over the years—oysters with melted espresso butter in Amsterdam, cascara chocolates in London—but those are hard to reproduce at home. It's better to go simple, and to think of coffee as something lovely to include alongside a good meal, like how you might think of sparkling water or wine—or just a dang cup of joe with a hamburger, or a piping-hot pot with a nice steak, à la Elmer Fudd.

Breakfast is the obvious place to start: try making your own overnight oats with almond milk and fresh fruit, and pairing that with a nice warm mug of your favorite brew. For a more classic pairing, there's something deeply primal and satisfying about the union of bacon, pancakes with maple syrup, and coffee, the very best version of which is available at a cafe in Paris called Holybelly (trust us).

Coffee tastes good with pretty much any form of bread, which means it pairs surprisingly well with something like a lunchtime turkey sandwich or grilled cheese. And at the dinner table, we like to incorporate coffee into the meal itself. Coffee grounds make for a wonderful element in a dry

Coffee grounds make for a wonderful added element to a BBQ dry rub.

rub for barbecue, or maybe try pouring a little brewed coffee into your homemade steak sauce. Above all else, in the evenings, a shot of espresso can make a wonderful bookend to a lovely meal: as an aperitif, it awakens the mind and palate for the meal to come—especially if paired with a little Campari and a side of soda water—and to finish off, perhaps float a bit of grappa over a shot of espresso, in a style the Italians call *caffé corretto*.

Coffee can be a love language.

When we talk about making coffee part of your home, we're talking about making coffee part of your life: the good and the bad. Coffee can definitely help comfort you in times of heartbreak—this is probably its own entire book, if we're honest—but we think the rituals and intentionality around coffee really shine when seen as part of its own love language. Whether that certain someone is staying the night for the first time or you just moved into a place together, coffee becomes part of the daily rhythm of your relationship. It's there with us through it all.

You might share a big pot together one morning over a Sunday stack of newspapers; you might brew up something for your partner to enjoy when they first get home from a long day of work. This is different for everyone, as personal as your own story, your own love. For partners with a new baby in the house, brewing coffee for each other is an act of mercy and kindness, a way of getting through the joys and tensions of kids together. For couples working high-stress jobs, making your partner a cup of coffee is like saying, "Hey, I got you. I love you."

Making coffee at home for the person you love is an expression of that love, and nothing else tastes as sweet.

> For partners with a new baby in the house, brewing coffee for each other is an act of mercy and kindness.

Coffee is a great reason to host a house party.

You've got your home brewing setup figured out, with some cute cups and a couple of food ideas, so why not put it all together and host some of your friends? Springtime in the garden, bundled up by the fire in winter—any old Saturday will do. Brew up enough for everyone and make sure you've got some extra for refills. Cakes and pastries are a natural approach here, and though pairing pastry and coffee is a theme in many cuisines (hello, Austria and France!), we especially like those that draw from the Scandinavian tradition of *fika*: the Swedish midday coffee break. Put out some nice cardamom buns, invite some friends over, keep the coffee pouring, and let the conversation flow.

Brew up enough for everyone and make sure you've got some extra for refills.

3

RULES FOR
THE CAFE

There's never been a better time to enjoy quality coffee.

We live in the golden age of coffee. There has never been more access to great, quality coffee than there is right now. But how can you tell the good from the bad?

Fortunately, we live in a time when just about every city in the country has a cafe serving and selling incredible coffee, and a local roastery to provide you good-quality beans to brew at home. Start with finding the best cafe in your city and let its staff be your guides.

RULE 30

There has never been more access to great, quality coffee than there is right now.

The history of the cafe is social.

RULE 31

From the sixteenth-century Ottoman coffeehouses of Istanbul to the eighteenth-century Enlightenment cafes of London to the nineteenth-century revolutionary salons of Paris to the twentieth-century beatnik bars of New York and San Francisco, cafes have always been a social space, and as such, a great catalyst for social evolution. At Cafe Novelty in Salamanca, Spain, writer Gonzalo Torrente Ballester is held as a sort of patron saint of cafe camping—that is, hanging out for indefinite periods of time—so much so that he has literally been enshrined by the cafe in the form of a sculpture, permanently occupying his favorite seat in the cafe. The French Revolution was fomented in cafes, and the Age of Enlightenment never would have happened without cafes for people to hang out in and discuss liberty and fraternity. The international insurance market Lloyd's of London was founded in a cafe, and so was Instagram. The cafe as a social space isn't changing anytime soon.

> The Age of Enlightenment never would have happened without cafes for people to hang out in and discuss liberty and fraternity.

The cafe's role is evolving.

And yet, we see the role of the cafe starting to change within society, as the space shifts from merely a conduit for social interaction—fueled by endless cups—into something capable of culinary greatness, of providing thought-provoking and deeply evocative sensory experiences. Sixteenth- and seventeenth-century cafes were, above all, about the people. Today's cafes are about the people too, but it's also about the coffee now, in equal measure. As coffee gets better and more delicious, the cafe is reclaimed as a focal point for expressing what coffee can be. A social lubricant, yes, but also a culinary experience capable of taking you around the world in a single cup.

RULE 32

Today's cafes are about the people and coffee in equal measure.

Your barista is your chef, server, and therapist.

RULE 33

It's kind of a weird gig, when you think about it! When you walk up to the bar in a modern cafe, it's a barista behind the register who takes your order (this is just the register part of their shift). Then it's a barista who physically creates the drink you've selected, combining diffuse ingredients in a style not unlike that of a great bartender or chef. While all this is happening, you might chat with the staff about your day—where you're headed after coffee, how you're feeling about that big work presentation, or what your kid dressed as for Halloween.

There is no real demarcation of labor—the server is the chef is the maître d'. It's a hybrid role that can be incredibly demanding for those who perform it, and it requires a tremendous amount of emotional labor and social IQ to survive. And yet there are those who love it. It's an exhausting and exhilarating job, and we feel strongly that the negative stereotypes around baristas—while sometimes totally true (see Rule 35)—should be countered with a more rounded appreciation and empathy toward the barista.

> Being a barista requires a tremendous amount of emotional labor and social IQ.

Being a barista isn't especially hard, but being a good barista—one who can balance the social needs of the role with a laser-focused execution that honors the coffee itself—is a high-wire act of the highest order.

Please always tip your barista.

Baristas in America rely on tips to make up a portion of their wages, same as a bartender or restaurant server. For better or worse, tips are the lifeblood of the American service economy, and you need to participate if you want to enjoy things like a nice cup of coffee. Those tips often go straight back into the neighborhood economy, at the sandwich spot down the street, the bar across the way, the record shop or the convenience store.

How much should you tip? A dollar per drink is our standard. Like drinks at a bar, the $1 per drink smooths out some disparities between how long each individual drink takes to craft, and you wind up with a fair average. A quick cup of coffee to go from a batch-brewed urn? $1 per cup. A carefully brewed pour-over coffee that took five minutes of focused intention? $1 per cup. The same as you'd tip for a beer or a cocktail.

Tips often go straight back into the neighborhood economy.

You might be wondering, what about places in the world where tipping is not the norm? We aren't asking you to rewrite social norms in the name of coffee service workers. Tipping is much less common in Asia, Australia, and Europe, and there's a lot of reasons for that (social safety nets, different approaches to a living wage, and so on). But if you're reading this as an American and wondering if the rules apply to you abroad, we suggest you stick with that $1 average. Nothing helps dispel the ugly American stereotype abroad like politely tipping even when it's not expected. Tipping might not be the norm around the world, but it's still often appreciated.

The snotty barista trope is real— for a reason.

RULE 35

Now that we've established the degree of difficulty it takes to be a great barista and why this should be respected, it's fair to talk about what happens when it all goes wrong. The snotty barista trope has been portrayed in film and TV for decades, and we think it has some legitimate root causes, which we'll elucidate below.

Being exposed to an endless stream of social interactions is exhausting, and that exhaustion can present as an aloof or snobby attitude. Baristas have not traditionally been respected the same way one might respect a craft bartender or chef. It can feel to the baristas we've talked to that the question is always looming: "What do you *really* want to do instead of this?"

> It can feel to the baristas we've talked to that the question is always looming: "What do you *really* want to do instead of this?"

The portrayal of snobby and condescending baristas in the media and cafes that reinforce these stereotypes with the behavior of their own staff, creates a sort of feedback loop that impresses these stereotypes on the next generation of baristas. It really is a hard, underpaid job that's demanding in terms of emotional labor, physical labor, early morning shifts, and unprofessional environments. Many cafes are the smallest of small businesses, run without a clear hierarchy, often owned and operated by people without much experience. It's a milieu that can breed resentment, which feeds back into that snotty trope.

Basically, we're saying that if this were the environment you found yourself in, you might be snotty too. A little compassion and empathy goes a long way, and we're happy to follow this bummer rule up with some good news to cleanse the palate.

The snotty barista trope is dying.

RULE 36

The problems we talked about in the rule preceding this one (that's Rule 35) are still going on today, but happily we can report that, by and large, the snotty barista trope is on its way out. There are several reasons why—some obvious, others less so.

Baristas are slowly earning more respect, as coffee is given pride of place at top restaurants around the world. When chefs like René Redzepi (Noma) and restaurateurs like Danny Meyer (Union Square Hospitality Group) make their coffee programs a point of emphasis, this trickles down to the wider public consciousness of coffee being something culinary and special, more than mere fuel. Similarly, news stories like the one about Blue Bottle Coffee selling for $500 million help signify that progressive coffee has arrived and should be taken seriously.

Customer service is a major factor in a cafe's ability to survive.

Delicious coffee is becoming more ubiquitous, and thus more normalized. When you're the first quality-focused coffee bar in town, it can be hard to get people to respect you, which can breed resentment among the staff. But when there are five shops just like yours on the same street, people are going to approach what you're doing from a place of familiarity and respect.

As the market becomes more crowded, customer service is a major factor in a cafe's ability to survive. Business is booming and people love your drinks— there simply isn't time to be snotty, and there are plenty of other options to seek out if you are.

This is a big concept to unpack and could perhaps be its own book, but in really broad terms, it seems like some of the wider cultural forces behind the Gen X snotty barista trope have died out as millennials have taken over the workforce. The culture is perhaps less angsty, or at least has repurposed its angst in more meaningful ways.

We see the snotty barista less and less in our travels to cafes around the world and hope your experience is the same. If the last time you received snotty barista service it was soundtracked by The Shins, let us suggest you revisit your local coffee bar with clear eyes, an open heart, and surely better music.

The Weird World of Professional Barista Competitions

Modern barista competitions as we know them today started around the turn the millennium, with the first North American Barista Championship taking place in the year 2000. The classic format works like this: a fifteen-minute routine in which the competing barista must make a series of espresso shots, milk drinks (classically cappuccinos), and a signature beverage drawn from the bartending world (but not, paradoxically, containing alcohol). Over the last decade, the culture around these barista competitions has grown considerably, with many new events and formats advancing participation worldwide. Annual tournaments take place today in places like London, New York, Melbourne, and Oslo.

Take it from us: Sprudge has covered, live and in person, all kinds of coffee competitions—hundreds of hours of competitive coffee making, from Knoxville, Tennessee, to Santa Cruz, California; from Budapest, Hungary, to Bogota, Colombia, and all points in between. And over those years, we've learned a thing or three about just how funny and weird these events are.

These events are ostensibly skills-building workshops, but some tournaments also boast sizable cash prizes. Baristas will train for dozens, even hundreds of hours, working late into the night on honing their routines, developing perfectly repeatable cappuccinos and espresso shots. Signature drinks once meant plopping a bit of chocolate syrup into an Americano, but today they more closely resemble something you'd expect to be served at a Michelin restaurant. Dry ice is not uncommon, and we've seen vacuum tubes, smoke guns, spherification, sensory deprivation, and even powdered coffee substances for the judges to snort.

Every year brings new and bizarre variations on the tried-and-true base format: fifteen minutes, three sets of drinks, and a slavish attention to detail. It's like watching a dog show and MasterChef at the same time. They are funny, truly weird, and where the dark heart of nerdy innovation and change in the coffee industry beats strongest. Long may they live—dear Lord have we seen a lot of them—and we'll be back again no doubt.

One weird trick to finding a great cafe in any city.

RULE 37

Here's the truth: you can find the best place to drink coffee in almost any city and region on earth in about five seconds if you have ready access to the Internet. First go to Google, then type in the name of the city or region you're looking in along with the search term "Sprudge." Google will give you results from the Sprudge archives—during the last decade, we've employed hundreds of reporters around the world to find the good stuff for our readers. You won't find *every* cafe in a given city this way, but you will find the places offering unique and extraordinary coffee experiences that are worth your time and money.

Yes, we're aware it's cheeky for us to say, "Just look at Sprudge," but it's a fact-based assertion. Chances are, you'll find what you're looking for using this one weird trick.

> We've employed hundreds of reporters around the world to find the good stuff for our readers.

Baristas know all the coolest stuff in their neighborhood.

We've learned a happy lesson over the years: the best way to get to know a city is by starting with coffee. Find a good coffee bar, get something to drink (obviously, you should not simply use the cafe as a social space without making a purchase), then ask a local barista where to go. Chances are, the barista makes coffee for the city's best chefs, bartenders, shopkeepers, and gallerists, and if they don't know them by their name, they probably know them by their drink.

Your barista might be able to tell you the names of a few other cafes worth checking out, or know the best place to get lunch nearby, and they (or their colleagues) could point you in the direction of an interesting cocktail destination or a nice wine bar. Like a popular local bartender, baristas are connected to all kinds of good stuff in their professional community, rooted in their cafe's neighborhood. This makes them a tremendous resource if you want to get to know the city better.

Whatever it is you're looking for, the barista won't judge. Just be sure to read the moment first, and make sure they've got a second to chat. From there, it's as simple as saying, "Hey, I'm from out of town. Where should I go next?"

The barista makes coffee for the city's best chefs, bartenders, shopkeepers, and gallerists.

Please use your headphones.

We get it: this is your "coffice," a coffee bar in which you work on your laptop, sometimes for hours on end. There's nothing inherently wrong with this, as long as you tip considerately, order a new drink every hour or so, and treat the staff with respect. But you need to put on your headphones.

We do not want to listen to your podcast. You need to put on your headphones.

We do not want to watch the latest viral internet video with you. You need to put on your headphones.

It's about public courtesy, and really, it should be about dignity—for you, for us, for everyone.

We do not want to hear both sides of your Skype call. You need to put on your headphones. (Or even one side—you might consider stepping outside altogether to take the call.)

Your taste in music might indeed be interesting and cool, but you still need to put on your headphones.

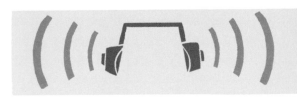

It's about public courtesy, and really, it should be about dignity—for you, for us, for everyone. Cohabitating a coffee bar space amplifies certain social mores; it should be the place where you are the *most* polite, not the least. And that extends to bringing in your own elaborate laptop rig, replete with mouse, and manspreading out (it's always men who do this) to occupy more than one table. It's enough already, and when you get called out, you'll deserve it.

We think cat videos are funny too. You can even send us the link so we can watch later. But for now, please mind yourself. Don't make the whole room uncomfortable. You can thank us later for helping you avoid an ugly scene, but for now, please just put on your headphones.

Small-town coffee can be really great.

RULE 40

Small-town coffeehouses have always been there, but today's raw materials—and especially quality green coffee, the raw coffee beans before they're roasted—have never been more readily available for budding coffee entrepreneurs. Remember, this stuff all comes from Ethiopia, Colombia, and other producing countries in the first place (see Rule 2); coffee does not discriminate against its final destination, be it Midtown Manhattan or Manhattan, Kansas. In small towns, the coffee quality can be just as good, for a fraction of the cost in bigger cities, and whether you're an owner, a patron just passing through, or an ardent regular, the ability to connect intimately with the local community is unmatched.

The coffee quality in small towns can be just as good, for a fraction of the cost in bigger cities.

Just as a small sampling, Chillicothe, Ohio (population 21,000) has Rost Coffee; Cottleville, Missouri (population 3,000) is home to VB Chocolate; Ipswich, Massachusetts (pop. 13,750) is home to Little Wolf Coffee; Nelsonville, Wisconsin (population 191) has Ruby Coffee Roasters; and Port Townsend, Washington (population 9,000) has the new Velocity. And it's not just the United States. The tiny parish of Udny, in rural Scotland, is home to Coffee Apothecary; the far-flung Faroe Islands have Brell Cafe; and the northern Norwegian town of Stjørdal is home to Langøra, a progressive and delicious coffee roasting company.

Big cities, small towns—we aren't so different. Everyone wants good coffee, and this is a trend that shows no sign of slowing.

Drink an espresso at the bar with the barista.

The barista role contains multitudes (see Rule 33) and your barista is likely to have their hands full with a number of different tasks. But if the cafe isn't slammed, and there's an area near the espresso machine with counter space, it's worth ordering a shot of espresso and enjoying it right there at the bar next to the barista. You might strike up a conversation with them, or get the opportunity to give a little feedback on the shot itself, or ask them questions about it. Indeed, at a good coffee bar, baristas are always tasting and tweaking the espresso they offer, and so this feedback will probably be requested directly by the barista. If you're still learning about coffee and what you like, this can also be a good chance to pick up something about the variables that went into making that shot. Have a chat; talk about what you taste in the cup; use this as a human moment to connect with the barista across the bar and say thank you by making some eye contact.

Have a chat; talk about what you taste in the cup.

Bussing your table is polite (but not always required).

Start by looking
around you: Are
there empty cups
on the other tables?

There's no standardized practice for bussing tables across cafes worldwide, but it is a good and polite thing for you to be thinking about at the end of your cafe experience. Start by looking around you: Are there empty cups on the other tables? Is there a visually obvious place for you to set down your cups for collection after drinking? In some cultures, table service at coffee bars is more common. Did a server bring out your coffee, or take a food order from you at the table? When in doubt, go ahead and bus your table unless explicitly told otherwise. Remember, your goal is to be maximally polite and mindful in a cafe setting.

Flavored coffee is usually gross.

Progressive cafes serve coffees with flavors of stone fruit, cherry, and lemon verbena. These are flavor notes gleaned from the coffee itself, made possible by the terroir, variety, processing, storing, and roasting. This is not what we're talking about when we talk about flavored coffee.

When we say flavored coffee, we're talking about coffee that is roasted and then infused with chemical bonding agents (propylene glycol) with natural and/or artificial flavorings. You won't find flavored coffee at most high-end cafes or roasters. But you know what? If you do come across some and happen to like it? That's fine. We aren't the flavor police.

Just a word to the wise, however: If you do choose to indulge in a nice bag of flavored coffee (a vanilla, perhaps, or even a taco flavor—yes, that exists), and you intend to brew that at home, you'll need to deep clean your equipment before running any other coffee through it. That's most especially the case for your grinder, where the flavors can get stuck in the oils released by the grinding process. If you're really a flavored coffee fan, it's a small price to pay for enjoying that hot mug of Buttered Rum Blend. For your humble authors, an occasional cheeky Dunkin' Donuts Hazelnut Delight on our trips back East is enough to satisfy our flavored coffee yearnings.

But you know what? We aren't the flavor police.

It's easy to deconstruct the coffee bar menu.

You can safely lump coffee beverages into two categories: brewed coffee and espresso coffee.

Brewed coffee is the ubiquitous brew one might add cream and sugar to. It's served at diners, banks, gas stations, and tire service centers across the United States. Brewed coffee traditionally comes out of percolators, flat-bottom filter coffee makers, and big commercial batch brewers.

It's served at nice coffee bars, too, but typically with a degree of quality control and attention to flavor that you wouldn't find at, say, the auto dealership waiting room. These days, in addition to batch-brewed drip coffee, you'll find baristas brewing coffee with all manner of single-serve devices: cone filter, AeroPress, Chemex, siphon, or even the regionally popular Woodneck filter coffee sock. The single serving (sometimes just called a pour-over) can be a good opportunity to try a particular coffee from a particular origin, and your cafe will probably have a menu of coffees to choose from if you want to go this route. Brewed coffee can be a blend or from a single lot from one area—heck, it can even come from a single farm. Ask your barista.

We say drink what you like.

Espresso coffee is the juice that skyrocketed the Starbucks generation and made latte a household term. Espresso is the main ingredient and can be served on its own as a shot. It's also served with water to make a brewed coffee–type of beverage commonly referred to as an Americano. And it's served with hot textured milk to make cappuccinos, lattes, flat whites (see Rule 50), piccolos, cortados, and gibraltars. See our handy guide on page 124 for these and other drinks you might find on a coffee bar menu.

And all of these espresso coffees can be made with flavored syrups. Vanilla and hazelnut are popular choices, and for a seasonal treat, a couple of pumps of pumpkin spice go a long way. A lot of people love these drinks; others are purists. We say drink what you like. Heck, why not? It's your world. We're just living in it.

The Coffee Bar Menu

ESPRESSO

HOT WATER

AMERICANO

FOAM

STEAMED MILK

ESPRESSO

CAPPUCCINO

TEXTURED MILK

ESPRESSO

CORTADO

STEAMED MILK

CHOCOLATE

ESPRESSO

MOCHA

RED EYE

MACCHIATO

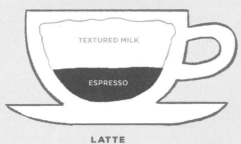

LATTE

ESPRESSO

Let your coffee cool down a little bit.

Extra-hot coffee is a strangely prevalent phenomenon in our go-go coffee world. We're here to tell you that extra hot coffee might not be all that great.

Your piping-hot coffee might be a warm comfort on a cold morning, but let us gently advise you: a bit of cooldown time is really for the best. When coffee is hot, not only is it a danger to yourself and others, but it's also nearly impossible to taste anything because heat dampens our ability to detect flavor. At temperatures between 120°F and 140°F, your flavor receptors will be able to pick out just how complex and dazzling coffee can be. In fact, coffee professionals grade coffee in what's known as a coffee cupping and only evaluate the taste after it has cooled off considerably—and many go back to these samples when the coffee is cold. Heat also degrades the natural sugars in milk, so that extra-hot cappuccino isn't going to be as sweet as it could— heck, *should* be!

Second, there are very real dangers inherent with hot beverages. When Stella Liebeck spilled hot McDonald's coffee in the early 1990s, many people only remember that she inadvertently catapulted the great

Coffee professionals evaluate the taste of coffee after it has cooled off considerably.

American tort debate. What many fail to realize is that she suffered horrific second- and third-degree burns on her body. And she didn't even ask for it extra hot!

Third, who are you to demand a specific temperature on your beverage? Kidding, kidding. Who are we to say you're wrong in liking hot and less flavorful coffee? You do you. Just be careful out there.

Drinking coffee at its hottest not only denies you the chance to taste coffee at its fullest, but it could also burn your mouth, or worse. So for the sake of safety and enjoyment, let your coffee cool off.

Milk sourcing matters.

RULE 46

"Excuse me, what's the name of the cow who provided the milk for my cappuccino?"

Think that's a silly question? It is. And yet, some baristas might be able to accurately answer it. On the World Barista Championship stage in 2013 (see page 108) Australia Barista Champion Matt Perger discussed the grazing habits of two clever cows named Freckles and Blossom. A year later, at the Big Eastern Barista Competition, Jenna Gotthelf described the "fantastic bovine lifestyle" of the High Lawn Farm cows that provided her cappuccino's milk.

Coffee professionals are focusing on milk quality, and dairies the world over are taking notice. Across the globe, small-scale farms are teaming up with cafes and roasters to develop milk that is made specifically for coffee. How? Altering the grazing patterns, diet, and conditions at the cow level can influence the chemical makeup of the milk. This can yield a milk with a flavor profile that complements coffee, or a milk with a different makeup of fats and proteins, one that is easier to steam and thereby makes cappuccinos and lattes more velvety.

Small-scale farms are teaming up with cafes and roasters to develop milk that is made specifically for coffee.

This kind of laserlike focus on milk just isn't possible with large-scale milk companies. Big dairy cooperatives may make a consistent product, but the smaller the dairy, the more interesting the milk tastes. That amazing cappuccino you had the last time you were in San Francisco? It might be because of the milk.

That's the milky way!

Alternative milks are delicious.

Coffee likes to keep pace with the modern world of food trends and can even act as a sort of canary in the coal mine. Awareness of food allergies is at an all-time high, and for this you might thank (or blame, depending on your outlook) the rise of the soy milk option in cafes.

RULE 47

Soy milk became synonymous with lattes back in the 1990s, thanks to its wide availability at chains like Starbucks. Unfortunately, steamed soy milk mixed with espresso is kind of gross. The texture isn't quite right, and the coffee winds up lost in the flavor mix. You might ask, "What have I done to deserve this dry, flavorless soy latte?" Fortunately, there have been significant advances in understanding how coffee interacts with alternative milks, and right now, we're living in a golden age for milk substitutes made from nuts and seeds, which flavor experts and coffee nerds agree taste far better than soy when steamed and mixed into coffee drinks.

We're living in a golden age for milk substitutes made from nuts and seeds.

There are now many fine alternative milks on offer at grocery stores here in the United States, including almond, pecan, and oat milks. And at the cafe level, it gets even more boutique. A recent survey of cafe nondairy milk offerings in Los Angeles revealed that

many of the city's best cafes—including Gjelina,
Go Get Em Tiger, and Bar Nine—are making their
own bespoke nut milks in-house, using ingredients
like pink Himalayan sea salt and pureed dates to
add depth of flavor.

As for us? We aren't big latte guys—sure, a mocha
is nice now and then (see Rule 51)—but we do like
exploring in-house artisanal nut-milk offerings
thusly: espresso, sparkling water, and a splash of nut
milk, in three separate glasses. It's a sort of decon-
structed latte—first invented in 2012 by Seattle's
Slate Coffee—but with smaller portions, and using
alternative milk. Give us a hazelnut and date milk
paired with a nice zippy espresso blend. Sip the 'spro,
then sip the nut milk . . . that's good! The sweetness
and textural complexity of each beverage bounce off
each other in a rather pleasing way. Enjoy the bubbles
last to refresh and repeat until happy.

Condiments are a right.

Condiment shaming made a brief attempt at relevancy in the early 2010s coffee scene, but most of those places are out of business now. Don't let snobs tell you that condiments—in coffee culture, this means milk, cream, and sweeteners, or even those flavored syrups you might request in your latte (see Rule 43)—are bad; we here at Sprudge would *never* tell anyone how to doctor their brew. And let's be real: Sometimes coffee absolutely needs a little help before it's palatable. Dark-roasted coffee with a little cream and a little sugar can make a sad cup into a joyful cup. Maybe even a little cinnamon? Don't get us started!

There are even many cultures where condiments like cream and sugar are an integral part of the coffee experience. In the classic espresso bars of Milan, your shot will be served alongside a complimentary packet of sugar, and it's not impolite to use it. In the Vietnamese coffee tradition, brewed coffee drips directly over sweetened condensed milk to make a *ca phe sua da*; if you've never tried one, you are in for a treat. In parts of the Middle East, coffee is ground with cardamom before brewing, and in Cuba, raw sugar is sometimes placed directly into the portafilter for a presweetened espresso shot.

In many cultures, condiments like cream and sugar are an integral part of the coffee experience.

None of these traditions is wrong or bad, and actually they're all pretty delicious. But like all things in life, a little compromise can go a long way. If you're at a fancy coffee bar in, say, New York City or Tokyo, you might consider trying your coffee straight up first before adding your desired condiments. That way you can experience the unaltered drink first before doing your thing to the rest of the cup. Who knows? Maybe a well-made latte or cup of brewed coffee will be naturally sweet enough for you to enjoy as is, no condiments required.

Coffee without cream and sugar might blow your mind.

There are some outstanding coffees being produced out there in the world, and then thoughtfully roasted and expertly brewed. Just like any well-stewarded and crafted culinary product, when coffee is cared for at every step of the supply chain, the final product can be life changing. Or if not life changing, just really very pleasing.

These are coffees that want nothing else: not cream, not sugar, not much more than a grateful consumer who appreciates how delicious it tastes. If you're in a really nice coffee bar and you order a cup of brewed coffee, just try it first without adding anything. Note how it tastes. See if you dig it. Then, if you need a comforting splash of something or other to cream things up, or just a pinch of sugar to get it to your liking, then by all means, do you.

When coffee is cared for at every step of the supply chain, the final product can be life changing.

The flat white does not exist.

The Flat White was invented by a barista in Australia. Or was it New Zealand? Many are sure, and many are certain, but all are wrong because the flat white does not exist. It is a misnomer, a fallacy, nothing more than espresso and steamed milk with a funny, catchy name that baristas must respond to now in cafes worldwide. It is a pointless antipodean import of little value or esteem. It is the Iggy Azalea of coffee drinks.

But wait, you might argue, a flat white is a specific kind of espresso and steamed milk. It has two shots, not one! It has a thin layer of foam (or no foam, depending on whom you ask). And it needs that little dollop point on the top to make it a *real* flat white, like how I saw it at Starbucks!

One might see it on a menu as a cortado, or a piccolo, or an SG-120. Truth is, it's just two ingredients put together to make a drink that goes by several names, with wildly varying volumes and ratios and milk textures served in an assortment of vessels. The flat white is just another name for these same drinks. It exists only as a concept; it is not an actual beverage.

One might see it on a menu as a cortado, or a piccolo, or an SG-120.

No matter where you find yourself in the world, whichever cafe you happen upon, the best practice is to read the menu and discover the offerings available. If you don't happen to find the flat white or the cortado or the gibraltar on the list, maybe use it as an opportunity for discovery. Or kindly ask your barista to make you whatever the hell it is you think a flat white is. Just know that what they're handing you will be indistinguishable from a small latte, which is what you really wanted in the first place.

A good mocha is a beautiful thing.

It's not an everyday thing for us. Or even an every-other-day thing. But once in a while, when the mood strikes and the scene is right, we like to indulge in that most indulgent of coffee bar treats: the mocha.

Oh! How the velvety whole milk dances with the cocoa. And wow! How those chocolaty depths meld into smooth ambrosia with the texture of espresso. Before you know it, the mocha is finished, an empty cup of chocolaty bliss gone too soon.

Of course, not all mochas are created equal. If you're gonna splurge financially (a good mocha is around $5) and calorically (the kind of mocha we dig is about 400 calories), you had better make it count. Good chocolate is just like good coffee, you know. It's grown by real people, exported around the world in a marvel of global commerce, and capable of expressing taste of place no different than coffee, wine, or cheese. We are *not* looking for a prepackaged, chemically coagulated chocolate-flavored syrup product of unknown provenance.

Oh! How the velvety whole milk dances with the cocoa.

So if you're going to indulge, we suggest seeking out a cafe making *really good* mochas, by which we mean a cafe using quality chocolate from a reputable chocolatier. Lauded chocolate brands like Dick Taylor Craft Chocolate (California), Askinosie Chocolate (Missouri), and Pump Street Bakery (United Kingdom) are working with cafes to make their chocolate mochas the best they can be. These mochas are made from powdered mixtures combined with milk and espresso in order to make the drink. Some cafes will even go an extra step and make their own ganache, melting down a chocolate bar and blending that with milk and espresso. Ask your favorite cafe how their mocha is built to learn more.

In the hands of a skilled and respected barista (and mixed with delicious local milk), the mocha can be a wondrous thing. The baristas at good cafes in your city will be happy to talk to you about the chocolate that goes into their drinks, and indeed, will be delighted that you asked. Cafes that go the extra mile to serve the real stuff are rightly proud of it.

In a heaven without consequences, we'd drink real mochas three times a day. Here on earth it's a special treat for the right kind of weekend morning, and ever so worth the wait.

4

RULES FOR A NEW COFFEE FUTURE

Coffee is probably good for you.

It feels like every week the news desk at Sprudge receives word of a new study: Coffee shown to stabilize brain waves! Coffee may lead to retina failure. Coffee might prolong your life! Coffee causes certain death. The studies come in one after the other, until as coffee lovers we experience a sort of data blindness amid a blizzard of contradicting information.

At least take some comfort in the fact that this is nothing new. Conflicting views of the health effects of coffee date back to at least the sixteenth century, when authorities warned that coffeehouses in the Middle East led to unseemly behavior and abnormal sexual practices. In seventeenth-century London, coffee shop owners posited coffee as a sort of cure-all, able to ameliorate stomach ailments, scurvy, and gout, and even help with childbirth. Later in the twentieth century, it was variously claimed that coffee can lead to poor school performance, stunt growth, and mess with your blood pressure. Now here in the early twenty-first century, new studies (and the study of studies) have led researchers to believe that coffee might help prevent a stroke (if you drink enough of it). Same goes for liver and prostate cancer, heart disease, and heart failure.

In the sixteenth century, authorities warned that coffeehouses in the Middle East led to unseemly behavior and abnormal sexual practices.

There will be more studies published in the time it takes us to write this book, with no end in sight—it must be an attractive field for scientists. But we're not sure you should be trusting big science to tell you what's good for you or not. If you've ever found comfort in the bottom of a nice hot mug, or used coffee as a practical stimulant to help you through your work morning, then you already know its benefits. Sometimes it's okay to trust your gut on this stuff. Coffee is absolutely, most definitely good for us. (Probably.)

Kopi Luwak is problematic.

The year was 2007. Filmmaker Rob Reiner's *The Bucket List* opened on Christmas Day, gifting the world with a charming buddy comedy. Unfortunately for coffee professionals, Reiner also inadvertently made Kopi Luwak a household name. Morgan Freeman introduces Jack Nicholson to the wildly expensive coffee that's been digested by a civet—a kind of Southeast Asian weasel. They have a laugh, and eventually Nicholson's character drinks it with gusto.

Since that fateful movie, Kopi Luwak has enjoyed an outsized place in the public imagination. Indeed, in taxi cabs and on airplanes around the world, the number one question that comes up when people find out we're in the coffee biz is something to the effect of, "Have you tried that cat/weasel/civet poop coffee?" The answer is yes, we've tried a few. And they were all disappointing.

Kopi Luwak is coffee that is processed not with water or heat but through the digestive tract of an animal: typically the aforementioned civet, called a *luwak* in Indonesia. And indeed, there are wild civets happily eating coffee cherries and happy farmers collecting droppings of undigested coffee seeds. The seeds are roasted and can be sold for over $300 a pound.

However, this tale does not reflect the total reality of Kopi Luwak production.

THE NEW RULES OF COFFEE

According to investigators at the BBC and other organizations, many Kopi Luwak producers keep their civets in cramped cages, force feeding them coffee cherries of varying quality. Not only is this an animal rights issue, the coffee it produces isn't very good. It's the opposite of the *gavage* practices that go into making foie gras—admittedly cruel, but with undeniably delicious results. Kopi Luwak has no such payoff. It's needlessly cruel and gross, gimmickry of the highest form, and as much as we might love Rob Reiner—especially early '90s *Sleepless in Seattle*-era "cute butt" Rob Reiner—we wish his movie hadn't mentioned it.

We don't recommend buying Kopi Luwak. There are world-class coffees that might not have the same novel approach to processing but are far better for your tastebuds, and most especially for the helpless animals, who didn't ask for any of this.

Coffee is a gateway drug.

RULE 53

Learning to love coffee is easy and delicious and offers a wide range of benefits, some expected, others more subtle. But when you get into thinking about some of the nuance behind coffee—the flavor spectrum and how we discuss it, coffee's journey around the world, and the artisans involved in every step of the process—you realize that there's something bigger happening. What looks like a brown cup of liquid to someone else becomes a Technicolor spectrum of flavors and aromas to a coffee lover, a complex expression of a thousand little variables influencing flavor. It is simultaneously both easy to love and endlessly complex, a deep dive you might spend your life happily exploring.

> What looks like a brown cup of liquid to someone else becomes a Technicolor spectrum of flavors and aromas to a coffee lover.

But along the way to becoming a coffee lover, you're subconsciously setting your brain and palate up for

sensory appreciation. Loving coffee is a gateway for falling in love with the flavors and expressions of a wide range of other delicious artisan products. Maybe you're particularly taken with how coffee can express a taste of place? Take that love and apply it to a product like cheese, which, in the hands of small cheesemakers working with heirloom breeds of cows, goats, and sheep, can so distinctly express taste of place and local traditions. Or maybe you're finding a lot of resonance in coffee's delicious utilitarianism, a mellow caffeine buzz that tastes great? You need to drink more tea, which has its own incredible world of cultivation and processing practices that yield a wide range of flavors and expressions. Access to remarkable small-lot teas in America right now has never been better. Brands like Kilogram Tea

(Chicago), Song Tea (San Francisco), and Spirit Tea (Chicago) are just a few of the new leaders in high-quality tea in America. If you love good coffee, you'll love what they're doing in the realm of *Camelia sinensis*. We could go on, but this is quite literally its own book.

For us, coffee has most especially been a gateway into wine, which as a beverage offers the same satisfaction to a map nerd, the same social convivial aspect, and a similar bottomless depth of knowledge to obtain and explore. It's also, like coffee, possible to enjoy wine quite happily without putting heaps of thought into the stuff, and there's no one way to do it. But we know for sure that our years of learning about coffee, drinking the stuff endlessly (both for fun and for work), and writing about it have primed us to be wine lovers. If you can appreciate the subtle nuance between a Colombia Cerro Azul gesha and a bourbon from Aida Batlle's famed Finca Kilimanjaro in El Salvador, the obvious and ringing flavor differences between a Syrah and a Riesling will womp you right on the nose.

Loving coffee is a gateway to loving so many other delicious things in our world. After all, humankind cannot live on coffee alone. (Though we've tried.)

Coffee loves you back.

Coffee is patient and kind. Coffee is not jealous, it does not brag, and it is not proud. Coffee is not rude, selfish, and it does not get upset with others—although your barista might get upset if you add cream and sugar without tasting it first. Coffee does not count up wrongs that have been done. Coffee takes no pleasure in evil but rejoices over the truth. Coffee patiently accepts all things—from a quick mug at the diner to a twenty-minute pour-over spectacle.

Coffee never ends. (You can just make more!) It is a gift of knowledge that begets never-ending curiosity: about the world, about ourselves, about perfecting your extraction ratio. But no coffee knowledge is perfect. There is only fleeting perfection—moments remembered forever, whispered quietly, invoking the heavens. In coffee we see a dim reflection of ourselves, as if looking into a mirror—imperfect, complex. You can know only a part of coffee, but never know it fully.

These things continue forever: hope, love, and coffee. And the greatest of these is love. But after that, coffee is definitely second. Or perhaps it's impossible to choose; perhaps these three things continue together in an eternal loop, forever filling and refilling until they runneth over. Hope, love, and coffee. We hope you know we'd love another cup.

These things continue forever: hope, love, and coffee.

Coffee can save the world.

The degree to which colonialism, resource extraction, inequitable global trade, and the ghastly rest of it are inextricably tied up with coffee is tough to parse. Coffee's narrative is a remnant of a time when great, powerful traders and statesmen—always men, almost always European—could point at a rudimentary world map, cast their eyes at a portfolio of cash crops, and say, "Let's plant this there."

Coffee is becoming more diverse and more inclusive.

This is changing, albeit slowly. Coffee producers are being looked to as artisans, not mere farmers. Awareness of the inequities of coffee trading has led to a focus on higher price points paid at origin, better sustainability and infrastructure development, and an increased awareness of coffee's long journey (and the many hands that touch it).

New leaders and voices are rising in the coffee industry for whom these issues are fundamental. Coffee is becoming more diverse and more inclusive. It's a neat microcosm for the wider societal and generational shifts we're living through together— racist pushback and presidential embarrassments notwithstanding. Coffee can make the world a better place, but it is also a pocket symphony in how the world is fast becoming a better place, fueled by coffee's deliciousness.

Acknowledgments

The authors would like to thank our families, our
parents, Sara and Dorothy Michelman, Ross
Martini, Anne Goldberg, Emily Timberlake, and
Lisa Schneller Bieser at Ten Speed Press, Kelsey
Wroten for bringing our words to life with your art,
Matthew Patrick Williams for technical support,
Terry Z for believing in us first, Duane Sorenson
for slipping us a $20 back in 2009, Aleco Chigounis
for the crucial introduction at Brumaire, Zac
Cadwalader, Robyn Brems, Liz Clayton, Gail O'Hara,
Michael Light, Erwin Chuk, RJ Joseph and all the team
at Sprudge, Junkie Bunny, Kimberly Clark, Murphy
Maxwell, Sam Penix, Katie Carguilo, Andrew Daday,
Jonathan Rubinstein, Scott Guglielmino, Helen
Russell and Brooke McDonnell, James Freeman,
Anastasia Chovan, Cosimo Libardo, Brant Curtis,
Jeffrey Young and Ludovic Rossignol, Brett Cannon,
Michelle Johnson, Ro Tam and Misty Cumbie, our
gifted photographer Jeremy Hernandez, Nicholas Cho,
Oliver Strand, Emily Yoshida, House of Intuition,
Lou Amdur at Lou Wine, Maru Coffee and Go Get Em
Tiger for caffeination during the production of this
book, everyone who let us crash on their couch over
the last decade of Sprudge (but especially Patrick
Berning), Fajr Wilson, Kelsey Wardlow, Char and
John at the Usual, and the city of Tacoma, Washington.

Index

COFFEE (*CONTINUED*)